Boudicca

Brian Williams

Heinemann
LIBRARY

www.heinemann.co.uk/library

Visit our website to find out more information about **Heinemann** books.

To order:

☎ Phone 44 (0) 1865 888112

📄 Send a fax to 44 (0) 1865 314091

🖥 Visit the Heinemann Bookshop at **www.heinemann.co.uk/library** to browse our catalogue and order online.

Heinemann Libraryis an imprint of Pearson Education Limited, a company incorporated in England and Wales having its registered office at Edinburgh Gate, Harlow, Essex, CM20 2JE – Registered company number: 00872828
"Heinemann" is a registered trademark of Pearson Education Limited
Text © Pearson Education Limited 2009
First published in hardback in 2009

Edited by Catherine Clarke and Rachel Howells
Designed by Kimberly R. Miracle, Jennifer Lacki, and Betsy Wernert
Original illustrations© Pearson Education Ltd
Illustrations by Mapping Specialists
Picture research by Elizabeth Alexander
Originated by Modern Age
Printed and bound in China by Leo Paper Group

ISBN 978 0 431 04475 0 (hardback)
13 12 11 10 09
10 9 8 7 6 5 4 3 2 1

British Library Cataloguing in Publication Data
Williams, Brian, 1943-
    Boudicca. - (Levelled biographies)
    936.2'04'092
A full catalogue record for this book is available from the British Library.

Acknowledgements
We would like to thank the following for permission to reproduce photographs: © Alamy pp. **11** (Mike Lane), **12** (Mary Evans Picture Library), **15** (Holmes Garden Photos), **26** (Brian Atkinson), **27** (Rodger Tamblyn), **28** (Jochen Tack), **29** (Rolf Richardson), **37** (Detail Heritage); © Ancient Art & Architecture Collection Ltd. p. **13** (M. Andrews); © Colchester Archaeological Trust p. **31 bottom**; © Corbis pp. **7**, **8**, **35** (Werner Forman), **10** (Angelo Hornak), **23** (Bettmann), **40** (Peter Adams/Zefa), **41** Roger Halls/Cordaiy Photo Library Ltd); © Getty Images p. **9** (National Geographic); © Museum of London pp. **19–21**, **31 top**, **33**; © Norwich Castle Museum and Art Gallery pp. **17**, **24**; © Rex Features p. **38** (Simon Roberts); © The Bridgeman Art Library pp. **4** (private collection), **14** (Louvre, Paris), **32** (Museum of London); © The Trustees of the British Museum p. **18**.

Cover photograph of Boudicca statue reproduced with the permission of ©Alamy (Johnny Greig Travel Photography).

We would like to thank Nancy Harris for her invaluable help in the preparation of this book.

Every effort has been made to contact copyright holders of any material reproduced in this book. Any omissions will be rectified in subsequent printings if notice is given to the publisher.

CONTENTS

Some words are shown in bold, **like this**. You can find out what they mean by looking in the glossary.

Warrior queen

Boadicea, Queen of the Iceni

Boudicca was a British queen who fought the ancient **Romans** 2,000 years ago. Many people know her name (it is sometimes spelled Boadicea). Boudicca led her army against the Romans, who had invaded Britain, but she was defeated, and died soon after her last battle. She could not prevent the Romans conquering Britain, but she remains a British heroine.

There are no pictures of Boudicca made in her lifetime. This picture was made in 1815.

The Roman Empire

The Roman **Empire** was at its biggest in 100 CE – about 40 years after Boudicca. In many lands, families under Roman rule copied Roman ways and obeyed Roman laws. The Roman army kept the peace. Romans, and people born in other lands, could be citizens of the empire, with special rights and privileges.

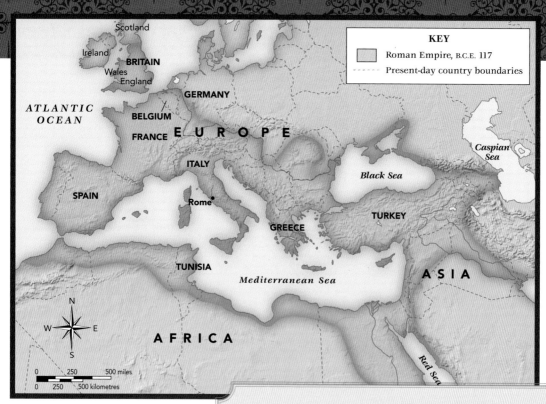

The city of Rome was the centre of the Roman Empire.
Until 43 CE, Britain was outside the Roman world.

Boudicca's people

History and **archaeology** tell us about Boudicca's Britain and its people.
Roman historians wrote about her and archaeologists have found out
more. Most of this book is based on this evidence, with a little imagination
to fill in some of the gaps in the story.

Boudicca was born around 30 CE. When she was about 18, she became
queen of the Iceni. The Iceni were a **tribe** who lived in Norfolk and
Suffolk in eastern England. In 43 CE, the Romans invaded Britain. Some
British tribes fought the Romans, and lost. The Iceni were friendly to
Rome until 60 CE, when Boudicca led them in a **revolt**. The Romans
defeated Boudicca around 61 CE, and after that they ruled much of Britain
for the next 400 years.

The letters BCE are used for all the dates before the Christian religion began.
BCE dates are always counted backwards. CE is used for all the dates after the
Christian religion began. CE dates always go forward.

Boudicca's Britain

The Iceni were one of the biggest **tribes** in Britain. Each tribe had its own land or territory. Many of these people were **Celts**, and their **ancestors** had crossed the sea from Europe to settle in Britain. These **migrations** happened during the **Iron Age**, when weapons and tools were made from iron for the first time. The Iron Age began in Britain before 700 BCE.

Boudicca probably grew up in a village in eastern England. Historians do not know who her parents were, but her father was almost certainly a **chieftain** and a **warrior**. Tribes were led by chieftains, and a strong chieftain might call himself a king.

Britain was a jigsaw of tribes. The names of tribes are those used by the Romans. The strongest tribes included the Catuvellauni and Boudicca's Iceni.

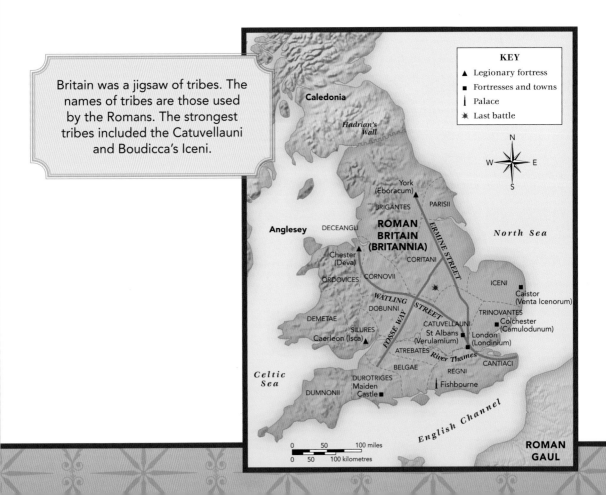

KEY
▲ Legionary fortress
■ Fortresses and towns
⌐ Palace
✳ Last battle

Caledonia

Hadrian's Wall

York (Eboracum)

BRIGANTES   PARISII

Anglesey   DECEANGLI

ROMAN BRITAIN (BRITANNIA)

North Sea

Chester (Deva)
CORITANI

ORDOVICES   CORNOVII

ICENI

Caistor (Venta Icenorum)

WATLING STREET
DOBUNNI

TRINOVANTES

DEMETAE

CATUVELLAUNI
Colchester (Camulodunum)

SILURES
Caerleon (Isca)

St Albans (Verulamium)
London (Londinium)

ATREBATES   River Thames

ERMINE STREET

FOSSE WAY

BELGAE   REGNI   CANTIACI

Celtic Sea

DUROTRIGES
Maiden Castle

Fishbourne

DUMNONII

English Channel

0   50   100 miles
0   50   100 kilometres

ROMAN GAUL

Kings and warriors

A king needed an army of warriors to fight for him. The king rewarded his warriors with gifts, after they fought for him. After a battle there was a feast to celebrate. When a roast ox or deer was brought in, the bravest warrior cut the first slice of meat. If someone else stood up to challenge him, there could be a fight, to see who was the strongest. The Celts were skilled at fighting – even women joined in.

Warlike women

Plutarch (lived around 46–120 CE), a Greek writer, described a battle between Romans and Celts 100 years before Boudicca was born. In this battle, Celtic women fought alongside the men. The Romans were horrified by the warlike women. They compared Celtic women to Amazons, the female warriors of ancient Greek stories.

Traders across the sea

The Iceni lived near the coast, and built ships. They became rich through **trade**. Iceni ships sailed across the North Sea to **Gaul**, which was part of the **Roman Empire**. The traders sold gold, wheat, cattle, and slaves. They came home with Roman pottery, wine, and jewellery. Boudicca's family was probably rich.

This is a Celtic pot. British Celts traded for Roman pots, but made their own too.

This is a modern recreation of an Iron Age Celtic house, the kind that Boudicca knew well.

Home life

An Iceni village had strong defences, to keep farm animals safe from wild animals, and to make it difficult for enemy warriors to sneak up and steal cattle or burn homes. The people surrounded their homes with an earth bank and ditch, and a strong wooden fence. Each family house had a **thatched** roof, and walls made from wattle (woven twigs), and daub (mud stuck over the twigs). It was dark inside, because the house had no windows. At times it could get smoky because a fire of **peat** or logs burned on the floor.

Most people in Britain were farmers. They grew wheat, oats, and rye (to make bread and porridge) and barley (to make beer, a favourite drink). From animal bones found in old rubbish pits, **archaeologists** know farmers kept cattle, pigs, and sheep. People wove sheep wool into cloth and used it to make clothes, which they dyed bright colours.

Celtic skills

Some people had special skills: they were good at hunting or making boats. Smiths forged swords and farm tools from metal. Celts mainly used **bronze** and **iron**. Metal-workers also made gold coins and gold jewellery, such as **torcs** (neck rings).

The Celts liked to paint their skins, with wiggly lines and circles. Men liked spiky hair styles too, stiffened with lime and clay. People added swirling patterns to things they made, such as clay pots, dishes, daggers, and **shields**.

Animals around the farm

Celtic farm cattle were small, sturdy animals. They provided meat and milk and were used to pull carts and ploughs. Celts loved horses because they pulled **chariots**, and were also used for races. The Celts also liked dogs, especially hunting dogs used to chase deer and other wild animals.

The Celts loved ornaments, especially gold torcs or neck rings.

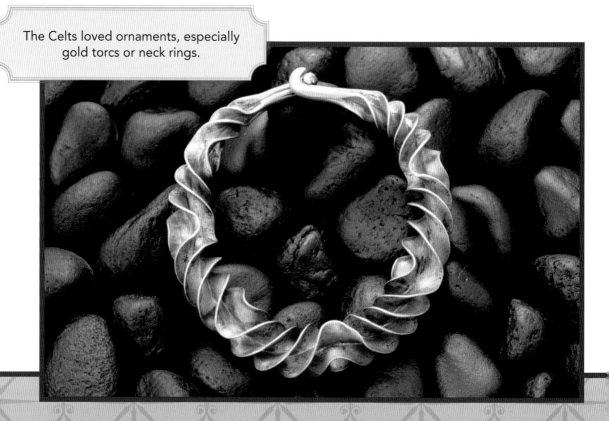

Growing up

As a child, Boudicca may have had a different name. Boudiga, or Boudicca, was the name of a Celtic **goddess** of victory. It is possible that the Iceni gave her this name after she fought the Romans.

She grew up in a world in which kings ruled, warriors fought, and slaves did the hardest work. The Celts were famous for their physical size, their love of fighting, and their bravery. A Roman historian, Diodorus Siculus, wrote that "the women are nearly as tall as the men, whom they rival in courage". Boys were trained to be warriors.

Neighbours at war

British tribes often fought one another. A tribe would raid its neighbours to steal cattle, gold, and slaves. Boudicca may have watched chained captives being brought to the Iceni camp. When the Iceni were under attack, she may have had to run for safety into a **fort**.

Maiden Castle in Dorset was a very large hill fort, so big that the Romans, who captured it around 44 CE, called it a town. This photograph shows how the area looks now — the actual fort is no longer there.

Celts and Romans hunted wild boars with dogs and spears. They did this both for meat, and for sport.

Forts were built on hilltops. From high up, lookouts could see an enemy coming. It was harder for enemy soldiers to attack uphill. There were hundreds of hill forts in Britain. Some forts were like small towns, with people living in them all the time. Others were used in wartime, as a safe place for people and farm animals.

Wild Britain

Boudicca's Britain was very different from Britain today. Much of the land was covered with thick forest. There were no roads. Travellers followed trails winding through the forests and along the ridges of hills. In the forests lived deer, wild boar, and fierce giant cattle called aurochs.

INVASION

The **Romans** first came to Britain 80 years before Boudicca was born. The Roman **general**, Julius Caesar, came from **Gaul** with 80 ships. It was not a successful trip but he returned the next year (54 BCE), with 800 ships. This time the Romans fought the British **tribes**, before sailing back to Gaul.

Rome learns about Britain

Romans and Britons got to know one another better through **trade**. British traders went to Gaul, and brought back Roman goods and ideas. The Romans found out how wealthy Britain was – it had wheat, gold, and tin. **Emperor** Claudius sent an army to invade Britain in 43 CE.

What the Romans tell us

Most of what is known about the Roman invasions of Britain comes from Roman history writers, such as Cornelius Tacitus (right). He wrote two histories of the Roman Empire, covering the years 14–96 CE. Two other writers who wrote about Britain were Julius Caesar, and Dio Cassius. Caesar was the only one who actually visited Britain.

A good time to attack

The Romans chose a good time to attack. Britain's strongest king, Cunobelinus of the Catuvellauni, had died. Without a strong person to command them, the British tribes were not likely to help one another. They were constantly fighting each other.

The Romans crossed the sea from Gaul, landed in Kent, and marched inland. They captured the British town of Camulodunum (Colchester). The Iceni stayed out of the fighting. The Romans said that if the Iceni did not fight they could go on trading and their lands would be safe. The Iceni agreed, so the Roman army marched to the north and west of Britain.

This carving from a tomb shows Roman soldiers fighting Celts in Gaul. The Romans are winning.

The Romans attack

Four Roman **legions** took part in the invasion of Britain, and were led by a general called Aulus Plautius. The invading army had about 40,000 men. Two sons of King Cunobelinus led the British **resistance**: their names were Togodumnus and Caratacus.

Surrender to the emperor

The Romans made Camulodunum their base. Emperor Claudius travelled from Rome to see Britain for himself. He rode in to Camulodunum on an elephant, to receive the surrender of 11 British kings. These were leaders who had been beaten or (like the Iceni) had not fought at all. Boudicca would have been about 13, and it is possible that she was there, watching the Roman victory parade.

Claudius (10 BCE–54 CE) ruled the Roman **Empire** from 41 CE until 54 CE. More interested in books than battles, he had never expected to become emperor.

The war moves on

There were fierce battles as Roman soldiers attacked British hill **forts**. One of the biggest battles was at Maiden Castle in Dorset. The Romans attacked the fort with giant catapults and crossbows. They set fire to the wooden gates and climbed over the steep banks and ditches. Many people in the fort ran away; those who stayed to fight were killed. The Romans set fire to farms and houses, and marched on to the next battle.

This is a **replica** scorpion, a small mechanical bow. The Romans used scorpions to attack British forts.

The invasion legions

The toughest and best-trained Roman soldiers belonged to a legion. Each legion had about 5,000 men. There were also other troops called "auxiliaries".

Living under Roman rule

By 47 CE an uneasy peace had settled over Roman Britain. The Iceni soon found out what this meant. By law, they could no longer carry weapons, except hunting knives. The Iceni were furious. They hid their best swords and spears, and handed in to the Romans only old rusty ones. The Romans also demanded the Iceni pay **taxes** to the Roman emperor.

In Celtic society, rank depended on birth, wealth, and bravery. Bad luck was also a factor. This picture shows (from left to right) a chieftain and his wife, a warrior, and a slave.

The Iceni revolt

After four years the Iceni had had enough of Roman rule. Out came hidden weapons, and they started a **revolt**. The new Roman **governor** of Britain, Ostorius Scapula, led the Roman army. The Iceni chose to fight in a narrow valley, where the Romans could not use **cavalry**. Scapula told his men to fight on foot. They won the battle, which was possibly fought in Cambridgeshire.

A new king

The Iceni chose a new king, Prasutagus. Around 48 CE, Boudicca married Prasutagus, and so became queen of the Iceni. Prasutagus wanted to keep the peace, and he and Boudicca met Roman officials. Her importance probably surprised the Romans. Celtic women had more freedom than Roman women. In Britain, husband and wife shared the family wealth. If the husband died, his wife inherited the wealth. In Rome, a wife could not inherit her husband's wealth, nor leave money to her children.

This Iceni coin was made during the reign of King Prasutagus. British **Celts** made coins that looked like Roman coins.

Roman Britain

In 54 CE, Rome had a new **emperor** – Nero. In 58 CE, **Roman** Britain got a new **governor**, Suetonius Paulinus. He was a tough **general** and he decided it was time to get rid of the **Druids**. The Druids were the tribal priests of Britain, and Boudicca knew how important they were. She may have known boys who became Druids.

Get rid of the Druids

Boudicca would have watched tribal ceremonies such as cutting mistletoe from a special oak tree with a gold knife. There were other bloodier ceremonies, and this is why the Romans hated the Druids. They feared the Druids' magic and horrible **sacrifices**. The Druids told **Celtic warriors** not to fear death in battle, because after dying, they would be born again. Suetonius hoped that if he got rid of the Druids, the British would stop fighting and become good Romans. So he led his army into North Wales, where the Druids had a refuge on the island of Anglesey. When the Romans attacked, everyone was killed.

The wild boar was the badge of the 20th (XX) Roman Legion. This clay tile was found in Wales, which tells us that the legion probably marched through Wales when the Romans attacked the Druids.

By 60 CE, the Romans had defeated or won over all the **tribes** of southern Britain. Only the far north (Scotland) was not under Roman rule. Celtic Britain was now Roman Britannia.

Sacrifices to the gods

The Celts believed in many gods – animal-gods, tree-gods, gods of rivers, pools, and mountains. To please the gods, priests left gifts at sacred places, such as ancient trees or deep pools. Sometimes they killed people (volunteers or captives) as sacrifices to the gods.

Some gods were part Roman, part Celtic. This is a statue of a Roman-British hunter god, with his dog.

A new world

The Britain the Iceni knew was changing. Roman soldiers were building roads and **forts**. The Iceni were being "Romanized". Prasutagus was still king, but his kingdom was run by Roman officials. Iceni settlements had new Roman names, such as Venta Icenorum ("market-place of the Iceni").

New towns

Camulodunum (Colchester) had become the centre of Roman government in Britain. It was only 18 years after the invasion, but the city had a town hall, a theatre, a temple, and shops selling Roman pottery. Londinium (London) was also changing, from a riverside village into a busy city.

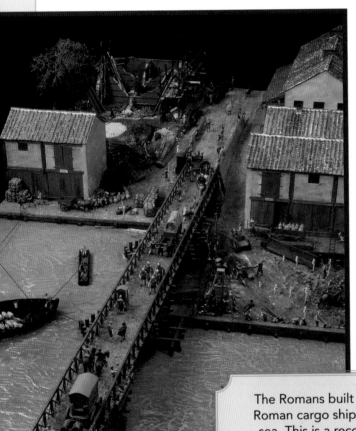

The Romans built the first London Bridge around 80 CE. Roman cargo ships sailed up the River Thames from the sea. This is a reconstruction of the riverside and ships, and shows how London Bridge might have looked.

Cogidubnus, a tribal king who lived in Sussex, was planning a Roman-style palace at Noviomagus (Chichester). It was not finished until after Boudicca died, but its remains can be seen today at Fishbourne. This is a drawing of how it looked.

Living the Roman way

Boudicca wondered what the future held in store for her family – she now had two daughters. Her husband, Prasutagus, was behaving like a Roman. His new house was filled with Roman-style furniture. Rich people had town houses and **villas**. Some were learning to read and write in **Latin**.

Roman towns

The Iceni had never lived in towns, like the Roman towns. A Roman town had a wall, with gates for people to go in and out. Inside were streets and squares. There were houses, shops, and even public baths. There were theatres too.

The king dies

Prasutagus died around 59 CE. His body was probably burned – **cremation** was a fairly new custom in Britain. Kings were usually buried in grave-mounds, with treasure, weapons, and even **chariots**. Prasutagus was rich. In his **will**, he left part of his land and wealth to the Roman emperor, Nero. He left the rest to his family.

Prasutagus thought that giving land and treasure to Nero would please Rome. He also felt that giving wealth to his daughters would attract powerful nobles as husbands. Boudicca might marry again. She was no more than 30 years old when Prasutagus died. Now she was sole ruler of the Iceni, until she or her daughters married.

The Romans see their chance

The Roman historian, Tacitus, says that Prasutagus hoped his will would stop the Romans taking more **taxes** from the Iceni. Decianus Catus was the Roman procurator (chief tax-collector). He said Prasutagus had no right to make such a will, and that the Iceni kingdom now belonged to Rome. Decianus Catus set out to claim Iceni for the emperor.

Roman roads

The Romans built roads from one army camp to the next. These camps were about 24 kilometres (15 miles) apart. Roman roads were built by soldiers from the **legions**, with local help. A Roman book lists the main roads in the Roman **Empire**. From it we know how long it took a horse-rider to get from town to town.

These Roman soldiers are shown on the move, carrying their **kit** on poles. When they left their ships the Roman soldiers marched for miles to reach their camp.

REBELLION!

Decianus Catus sent his taxmen and soldiers into the Iceni lands. They were told to seize the royal treasure. The **Romans** turned Iceni families out of their homes. They took horses and slaves, and led young Iceni men off to join the Roman army. Roman soldiers trampled through Boudicca's palace.

This hoard (hidden store) of Iceni coins was found in Suffolk. The owners of this treasure may have buried the coins to hide them from the Romans, or for safety during the rebellion.

Boudicca's flogging

Decianus Catus told Boudicca she owed more money, in return for the help the Romans had given Prasutagus. If she couldn't pay, she would be punished. The angry queen probably called her guards to chase the Romans out. The Romans hit back, by setting fire to Iceni villages. They arrested the queen. Then they stripped Boudicca naked, and whipped her, in front of her people. Such punishment was very painful, but also an insult. Boudicca's daughters were dragged off by Roman soldiers, and horrible stories quickly spread of what had been done to them.

Revenge!

As soon as Boudicca's daughters were returned, alive but sobbing, the Iceni went wild. They yelled for revenge. Men and women ran to get their hidden weapons. The Romans took to their heels. The Iceni killed a few, and took others prisoner.

The Iceni were going to war. They sharpened swords. They harnessed horses to the **chariots**. Off went messages to neighbouring **tribes**. It was time to forget old quarrels. Come and join Boudicca's Iceni and drive out the Romans!

United we stand

Boudicca is now famous for leading the Iceni in their **revolt**. Other leaders must have come to join her army, with their own **warriors**. The Trinovantes of Essex (see map on page 6) joined the revolt. The Romans wrote the history of the revolt. They saw Boudicca, the British queen, as their main enemy. It is her name that lives on.

The revolt begins

Some modern historians believe the revolt began in 60 CE. Tacitus says it was in 61 CE. It was probably spring. The Iceni planted no crops. They were going to war.

We can imagine Boudicca making a speech to her army, calling on the Iceni **ancestors** and the gods to help her defeat the Romans. This was probably when the Roman prisoners were killed, as human **sacrifices**. Within days, the army was on the move south. The Romans said there were 100,000 warriors, with women and children. No one really knows how many there were.

Roman gods

The Romans, like the **Celts**, had many gods. Statues of gods were kept in temples, and looked after by priests. The Romans made offerings to their gods, but did not kill people as sacrifices. This picture (right) shows a statue of Jupiter, the king of Roman gods.

Most of Colchester Castle was built after Boudicca's time, but it stands on stones that were once part of the temple that the Romans built.

The first town falls

The first target was Camulodunum (Colchester). The Romans had been building there for 10 years. Recapturing it would strike a blow at the Roman army, and encourage other tribes to join the revolt.

For the townspeople, the sight and sound of Boudicca's army must have been terrifying. Many of them fled. Those Romans who stayed to fight had no chance against such a huge army. When the Iceni charged through the streets, some Roman soldiers ran into the temple. They fought for two days until the Iceni broke in and killed them. The temple and the town were set on fire.

Britannia in danger

Roman Britain (Britannia) was in danger. News of the revolt spread as fast as a horse could gallop. What could the Romans do to stop Boudicca?

The Roman **governor**, Suetonius Paulinus, was at least three days' ride away, in North Wales. He sent orders to Petillius Cerialis, commander of the 9th **Legion**. He must stop Boudicca. The 9th Legion was probably in camp at Lincoln, but Cerialis did not take the whole legion with him. He rode out with as many men as he could gather quickly, a few hundred **infantry** soldiers and **cavalry**. When Boudicca's army came in sight, the Romans must have known they were doomed.

Roman legionaries looked like this, ready for battle. These men are wearing replica armour and holding shields and javelins.

This is a modern chariot race. The Romans had stopped using chariots in battle, but Boudicca probably had hundreds of chariots.

Boudicca spreads panic

It was a short, bloody battle and the few hundred Romans were cut to pieces. Only the cavalry got away alive, galloping for safety. Cerialis rode away, having seen the fearsome warrior-queen, later described by Tacitus (though no one knows how accurate he was). Tacitus says she was "very tall", spoke in a "harsh voice", and that "a great mass of red hair fell to her hips". Driven in a war-chariot at the head of her army, she spread panic wherever she went. Where would she strike next?

Chariots

Remains of British **chariots** have been found in graves so we know what they were like. They were made of woven sticks (wickerwork) on a strong wooden frame, and were very light. They had two wheels and were pulled by two horses. A chariot carried two people. One drove, the other jumped off, killed an enemy warrior, then jumped back on again. The Romans had chariots too, but only for transport and races.

LONDON BURNS

The **Roman** commander, Suetonius, rode for London, with his **cavalry**. The **legion** followed, marching down the Roman road later called Watling Street (see map on page 6). As soon as he got to London, the Roman **general** realised that he hadn't enough men to defend it. He may have expected to find more Roman soldiers in London. There were none. Only a legion would stand any chance against Boudicca.

People flee London

Scouts rode in with news: the British were coming. Many people fled, on foot or in carts, while others took to the river in boats. Suetonius pulled out too, leaving London to its fate, taking with his small force any who could join it, according to Tacitus. Anyone too slow to march with him – the old, women with small children, the sick – was left behind.

The massacre

What happened next was a **massacre**. Boudicca's army swept through London. Shocked Roman historians later reported that the British took no prisoners, but killed everyone. They set fire to wooden buildings. The flames could be seen for miles. Boudicca rode into the burning city, perhaps in her **chariot**, cheered by her **warriors**.

Many people in London were killed by Boudicca's warriors, and the city was burnt.

Buried evidence

Beneath the streets of modern London is a charred layer of burnt clay. This is all that is left of the houses Boudicca's army burned. The fire was so hot that the daub (clay) used as plaster on the walls hardened like **terracotta**.

L439

This helmet belonged to a Roman legionary, perhaps a soldier in London during Boudicca's revolt.

Into the brook

Boudicca's warriors flung heads, bodies, and weapons into the River Thames. The river was named after a **Celtic** god, so the warriors were making a **sacrifice**, to give thanks for victory. Skulls of people possibly killed by the Iceni were found in a London stream called the Walbrook. The skulls can now be seen in the Museum of London.

Boudicca could not stop the killing. Roman historian, Dio Cassius, wrote that her warriors hunted down and killed all noble "Roman" women. They probably killed anyone wearing Roman clothes. They hung dead bodies from poles and stuck them on sharpened wooden stakes. It was a horrible sight.

How the Romans saw it

The Romans could also be very cruel. They watched **gladiator** fights – for fun. Yet in their history of the **revolt**, Roman writers were shocked by so much killing. Instead of taking prisoners as slaves, Boudicca's warriors killed them. Why? Roman historians were trying to show the "non-Roman" British were barbarians, or enemies of civilized life. The truth was that the Romans did not realise how angry the Iceni were.

Head-hunting

Head-hunting was a Celtic custom. A Celtic warrior would challenge an enemy to single combat (one against one). The winner would cut off the head of the dead man, and take it home. It was a prize.

These human skulls were found in the bed of the Walbrook, a small stream that flowed through Roman London into the much bigger River Thames. Boudicca's warriors may have thrown in the heads of people they had killed, as a sacrifice to river-gods.

DEFEAT

From the still-smoking ruins of London, Boudicca led her army north.
She was heading for another **Roman** town, Verulamium (St Albans).
Its **Celtic** name was Verlamion, and it had been the capital of the
Catuvellauni **tribe**. It was now the third biggest Roman city in Britain.

The people of Verulamium knew that Boudicca was coming. Most of
them had left before she reached the city.

More flames and feasting

Boudicca's army did not have to fight to capture Verulamium. It was
almost deserted. They killed any townspeople they found, and then
started wrecking the city. They set fire to its new Roman buildings
and looted shops. Enraged, they overturned and smashed statues
of Roman gods and Roman **emperors**. They wanted to get rid of
anything Roman. Roman historians say that 70,000 people were killed
in the attacks on Colchester, London, and St Albans. The Iceni did not
keep count.

The next move?

As the Iceni celebrated their latest victory with feasts and songs,
some wondered what the army would do next. More prisoners had
been **sacrificed**, to ensure victory in battles to come. Iceni scouts
reported that Suetonius was camped in the Midlands, waiting for
legions to join him. There would soon be a battle. Boudicca and her
commanders must have talked late into the night, planning their next
move. The men prepared their weapons.

This bronze Celtic shield was found in the River Thames. It may have been thrown in as a gift to a river-god.

War-gear

Celtic **warriors** fought with a spear, a long sword, and a **shield**. They did not wear much armour. A Roman soldier wore armour made from leather and metal, and a metal helmet on his head. His main weapons were a short sword, a throwing spear or javelin, and he had a curved shield.

Into battle

Boudicca knew that it was not easy to command such a huge army. According to the Roman historian, Dio Cassius, she now led over 200,000 people. The army was too big to control, and Celtic warriors did not always obey orders.

Some of the British **chieftains** wanted to attack the Romans straightaway. Others wanted to wait. The next battle could settle the war. One more victory would end Roman rule in Britain.

The army began to move north. Its speed was slowed by thousands of women and children on foot. There were hundreds of wagons pulled by horses and oxen. Every day messengers rode in; the Romans were waiting.

A call for help

Suetonius had sent urgent orders for his legions to join him. He had retreated north of London into the Midlands, and now had about 10,000 soldiers. He was waiting for the 2nd Legion to come from Exeter, but its commander, Poenius Postumus, refused to leave the west. He may have feared that the western tribes would revolt too. Suetonius would have to make do with the army he had.

Romans liked to fight in lines, with shields together and swords ready to stab at the enemy.

Battle tactics

The British liked to fight hand to hand. Their favourite tactic was an **ambush**. In a big battle, they made a lot of noise, with drums, pipes, and yells, to scare the enemy. Then they charged, waving their swords and spears. The Romans were much more disciplined. Their soldiers were trained to stand in lines, shield next to shield. They waited for orders before throwing their javelins (spears). Then they moved forward in a solid mass to cut their way through the enemy.

This is how a TV film showed Boudicca charging into battle, standing in her **chariot**. The man on the right is the chariot driver.

The final battle

Suetonius was outnumbered. Boudicca's army was at least 10 times bigger. Suetonius chose his battlefield carefully. It was possibly in Warwickshire, but historians aren't sure. He drew up his troops in front of a wood at the top of a hill.

Before the battle

The Roman soldiers must have been worried when the British army appeared. Dio Cassius, the Roman historian, wrote that Boudicca was "very tall, in appearance most terrifying". She may have ridden out in front of her warriors. Tacitus made up a speech for her. She said she was not the first woman to lead a British army, and that, "on this spot we must either conquer or die with glory". Suetonius told his men to ignore "the savage uproar, the yells and shouts of undisciplined barbarians" and remember their training. Besides, he said, half the British army were women.

Unlike the Romans, the British did not wear armour. Some men stripped naked to fight, to show how brave they were. The Romans stood in lines, waiting.

The battle

With a tremendous roar, the British charged. The Romans threw their javelins (spears). Many Britons fell. The Roman began to advance and the Britons became jammed together, which meant they had no room to swing their long swords. The Roman **infantry** drove them back.

Tacitus says that 80,000 Britons were killed. Boudicca fled from the battlefield. Some sources say that she became ill, and died soon afterwards. The Romans said she killed herself, to avoid being taken prisoner. The **revolt** was over.

This table compares Iceni and Roman military strengths. For example, Boudicca had more soldiers (5 stars); the Romans only get ½ a star.

	Boudicca	Romans
Soldiers	★ ★ ★ ★ ★	⯪
Weapons	★ ★ ★ ★	★ ★ ★ ★ ★
Mobility	★ ★ ★	★ ★ ★ ★ ★
Armour	★	★ ★ ★ ★
Discipline		★ ★ ★ ★ ★

Boudicca Remembered

Roman historians claimed that only 400 Romans were killed in the battle. The Iceni fled back to their own territory in Norfolk. The Romans followed, seeking revenge. Captives were sold as slaves. Many people starved to death, because their farms had been burned.

After Boudicca

Boudicca was dead. Dio Cassius says her people gave her a secret burial, so her body may still be in a hidden tomb somewhere. One (probably untrue) story says she that is buried beneath Platform 8 at King's Cross Station. No one knows what happened to her daughters.

Hadrian's Wall took around six years to build, starting in 122 CE. It follows a line from the River Tyne in the east to the River Solway in the west.

A new Roman tax-collector arrived in Britain. His name was Julius Classicianus, and he treated the Britons more fairly. Suetonius was replaced by a less stern **governor**. Britons had to accept that they were now part of the Roman **Empire**. By 84 CE the Roman armies had moved into Scotland, though they did not conquer it. The Romans built Hadrian's Wall to defend Britannia – Roman Britain.

Remembered forever

Boudicca was not forgotten. Even the Romans admired her, and remembered her as a **freedom-fighter**. Roman writers used the **warrior** queen to point out faults in their own rulers. The Britons, and later the English, remembered her as a heroic fighter. This remarkable woman who went to war became a symbol of **resistance** against invasion and injustice.

Britain remained Roman until the 400s CE. Boudicca remained in people's memories – the warrior queen of the Iceni.

This statue of Boudicca stands in Westminster, London. It was made in 1902.

TIMELINES

Boudicca's life

30 CE   Possible date of Boudicca's birth. Christians believe this to be the year in which Jesus was crucified.

37   The Roman **emperor**, Tiberius, dies. The next emperor is the crazy Gaius, known as Caligula (a nickname meaning "little boot").

41   Caligula is assassinated. His uncle Claudius becomes emperor.

41 OR 42   King Cunobelinus, king of the Catuvellauni tribe and the most powerful leader in **Celtic** Britain, dies.

43   The **Romans** invade Britain. Roman soldiers capture key British settlements, including Camulodunum (Colchester).

43   Emperor Claudius visits Britain. The Iceni leaders and leaders of other **tribes** come to Camulodunum to accept Roman rule.

47   Prasutagus becomes king of the Iceni, after a failed uprising against the Romans. He is friendly to the Romans.

48 OR 49   Boudicca marries Prasutagus. They have two daughters. The Iceni live at peace with the Romans.

51   The British **resistance** leader, Caratacus, is captured and taken to Rome.

54   The Iceni hear that Emperor Claudius is dead. His wife, Agrippina, has her son Nero made emperor.

58   Suetonius Paulinus arrives to become **governor** of Roman Britain.

59   Nero has his mother murdered.

59 OR 60   Prasutagus dies. Boudicca becomes queen of the Iceni. Boudicca is ill-treated by Roman officials, as are her daughters.

60   Suetonius leads the Roman army against the **Druids** in Anglesey.

60–61   Boudicca leads the Iceni and Trinovantes in **revolt** against the Romans. The army burns three Roman cities, but is then defeated by Suetonius and the Roman army. Boudicca dies.

World timeline

10 CE	Cunobelinus of the Catuvellauni tribe is the strongest king in Britain.
14	The Roman emperor, Augustus, dies.
39	Adminius, a son of Cunobelinus, tries to persuade the Romans to invade Britain (because he has quarrelled with his family). The Romans never set sail.
41	Claudius becomes Roman emperor.
42	King Verica of the Atrebates tribe asks Rome for help against his enemy, Cunobelinus.
42	King Cunobelinus dies.
43	The Romans invade Britain. Claudius visits Britain for a victory ceremony at Camulodunum (Colchester).
47	Prasutagus becomes king of the Iceni. His wife is Boudicca.
47	The Iceni rise up in revolt after they are ordered by the Romans not to carry weapons, and to pay taxes. They are defeated by the Roman **general** Ostorius Scapula.
49	Romans create a settlement for retired soldiers in Colchester.
51	Caratacus, British resistance leader, is defeated in the west of England.
54	Emperor Claudius dies. He is succeeded by Nero.
Around 56	The Roman historian, Tacitus, is born.
58	Suetonius Paulinus becomes governor of Roman Britain.
60–61	The revolt of the Iceni, led by Queen Boudicca. Colchester, London, and St Albans are destroyed, but then Boudicca is defeated.
62	The Romans take their revenge by taking Iceni land and burning villages.
81	Agricola, governor of Roman Britain, leads the Roman army into Caledonia (Scotland).
100–110	The Roman Empire reaches its greatest size.
122	The building of Hadrian's Wall starts, to mark the northern frontier of Roman Britain.
150	The Roman historian, Dio Cassius, is born.
410	The last Roman soldiers leave Britain.
476	The Roman Empire comes to an end.

Glossary

ambush surprise attack by an enemy in hiding

ancestor grandparent or other distant relative

archaeology study of the past from remains, such as objects and evidence found underground or beneath the sea. The people who carry out this study are called archaeologists.

bronze metal made by mixing copper and tin; used to make weapons in ancient times

cavalry soldiers on horseback

Celts people living across ancient Europe, in different tribes

chariot two-wheeled light cart pulled by horses, used in battle

chieftain leader of a tribe or small group of fighting men

cremation disposal of a dead body by burning

Druids priests of the ancient Celtic religion

emperor supreme ruler of an empire

empire large area with many peoples living under the rule of an emperor

fort strongly defended place, with walls, banks, and other defences

freedom-fighter person who takes part in an armed rebellion against an enemy, in the hope of improving conditions. Boudicca is often remembered as a freedom fighter for the rebellion she led against the Roman government.

Gaul large area of western Europe including modern France, Belgium, and southern Germany. It was part of the Roman Empire.

general commander of an army

gladiator warrior trained to fight in the Roman arena for entertainment

goddess female god or supernatural being

governor ruler of a Roman province. A province was a territory conquered and ruled by the Romans, such as Britannia (Roman Britain).

infantry foot soldiers

iron metal used to make weapons and tools

Iron Age period during which a civilization makes most of its weapons and tools from iron; in Britain the Iron Age had begun by 700 BCE

kit belongings. The Romans wouldn't have been able to carry much in their kits, as they often had to march a long way to get from one army camp to the next.

Latin language spoken by the Romans

legion main battle unit of the Roman army, numbering at various times between 4,000 and 6,000 soldiers or legionaries

massacre slaughter of many hundreds or thousands of people

migration mass movement of people from one country to another, or across a country

peat partly rotten vegetable skin used to make fire

replica copy of an original object

resistance fighting back against enemies who have invaded a country

revolt uprising or rebellion against a ruler

Romans anyone who was a citizen of the Roman Empire was a Roman, not just people actually born in the city of Rome itself

sacrifices offerings made to a god or goddess; sacrifices could be treasures, flowers, oil or wine, dead animals, and even people

shield piece of military equipment, made of wood, leather, and metal, and carried by a soldier to protect his body

taxes money paid by people to a ruler or government

terracotta type of pottery made from clay and baked in an oven to harden it

thatched roofed with bundles of reeds or straw

torc metal neck ring, like a large bracelet, worn by Celts

trade buying goods and then selling them to make more money

tribe group of people sharing a similar way of life and beliefs

villa Roman country house or farm

warrior person trained to fight in war

will instructions about what a person wants done after his or her death

WANT TO KNOW MORE?

Books

Ancient Roman War and Weapons, Brian Williams (Heinemann Library, 2002)

Boudicca (Famous People, Famous Lives), Emma Fischel (Franklin Watts, 2002)

Invaders in Britain, Brian Williams (Pitkin, 2006)

The Life and World of Boudicca, Struan Reid (Heinemann Library, 2002)

The Romans in Britain, Brenda Williams (Pitkin, 2004)

Websites

www.bbc.co.uk/history/ancient/british_prehistory/iron_01.shtml
This shows a map of all the tribes in Britain at the time of Boudicca.

www.bbc.co.uk/history/historic_figures/boudicca.shtml
This site gives some basic information about Boudicca's life.

www.24hourmuseum.org.uk/norwich
Follow the link for local history to find information on Boudicca.

Places to visit

Butser Ancient Farm
Chalton Lane • Chalton • Waterlooville • Hampshire PO8 0BG
• Tel 023 9259 8838
www.butserancientfarm.co.uk
Using evidence from excavations of prehistoric and Roman sites, the farm
recreates life in the Iron Age when Boudicca led the Iceni to war.

Fishbourne Roman Palace
Salthill Road • Fishbourne, near Chichester • West Sussex • PO10 3QR
• Tel 01243 785 859
This is the finest Roman palace found in Britain. Visitors can see remains of
just some of its many rooms, and also the gardens, with recreations of Roman
life in Britain.

Iceni Village and Museum
Cockley Cley • Swaffham • Norfolk PE37 8AG • Tel 01760 721 339
This is a reconstruction of an Iceni village as it might have looked at the time
of Boudicca.

INDEX